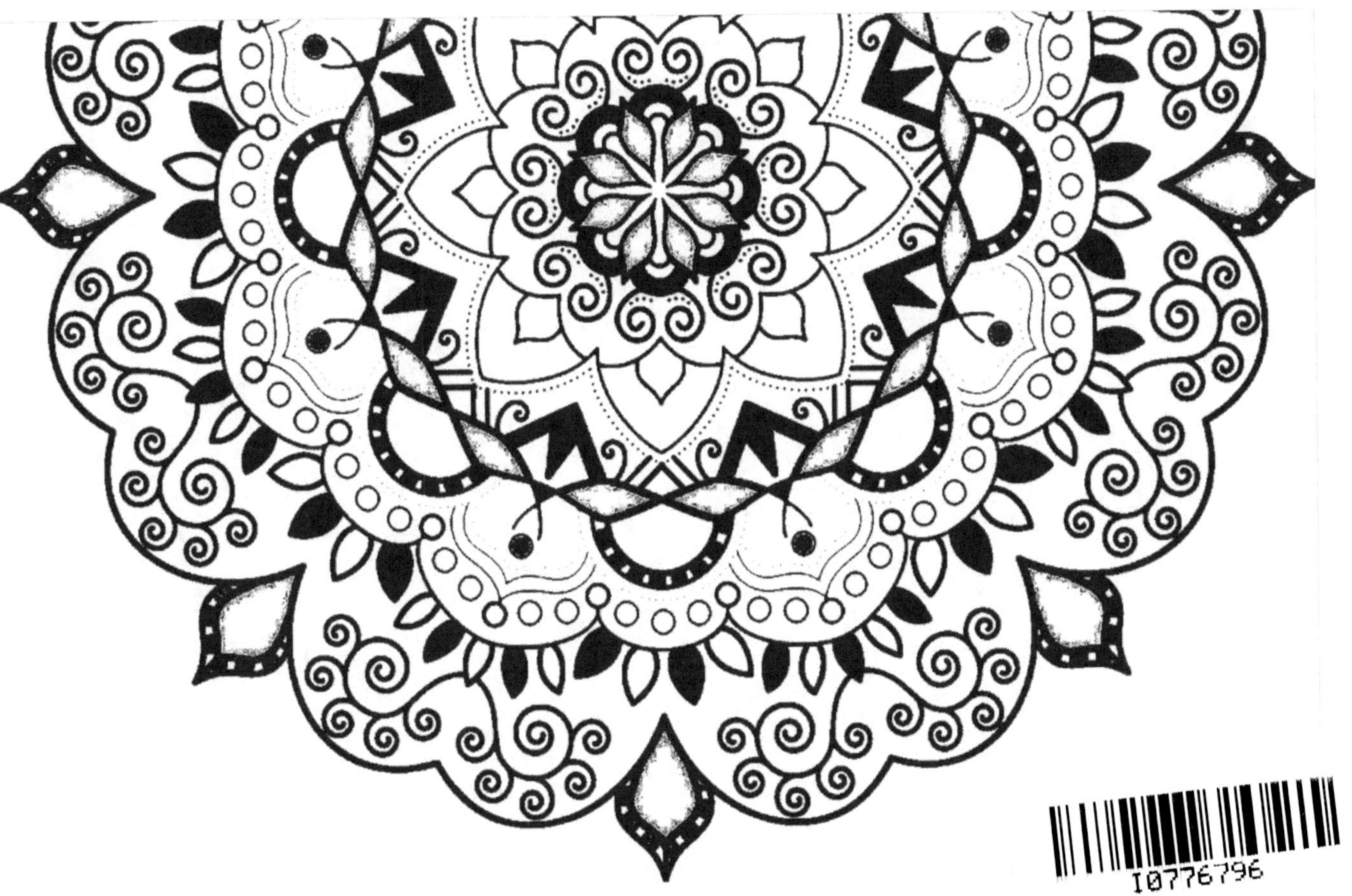

MANDALA WONDER

COLOR ART

Vanna Folliero

Mandala Wonder

COLOR ART

Copyright: Published in the United States by Vanna Folliero

Published NOVEMBER 2017

ISBN-13: 978-1979681452

ISBN-10: 1979681457

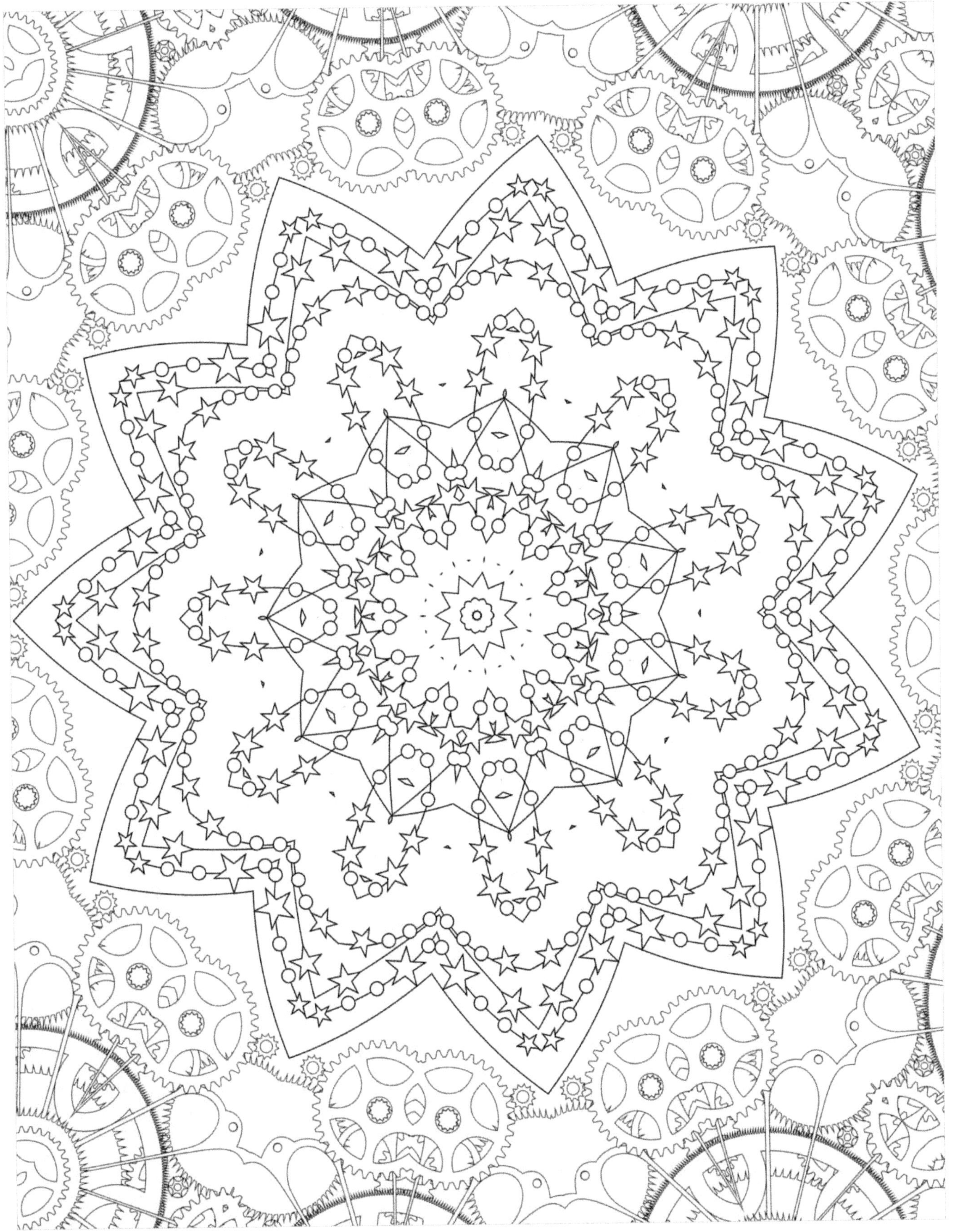

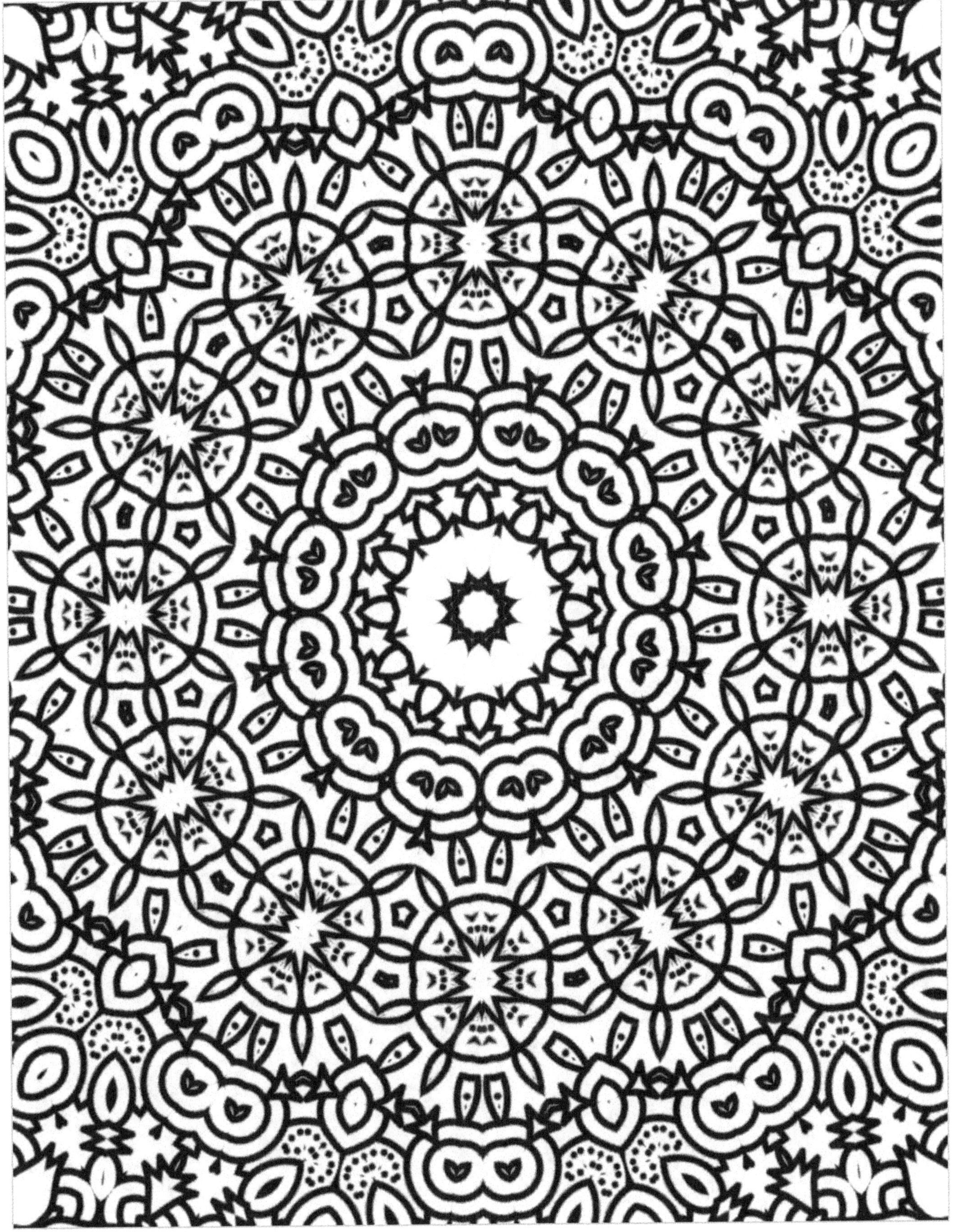

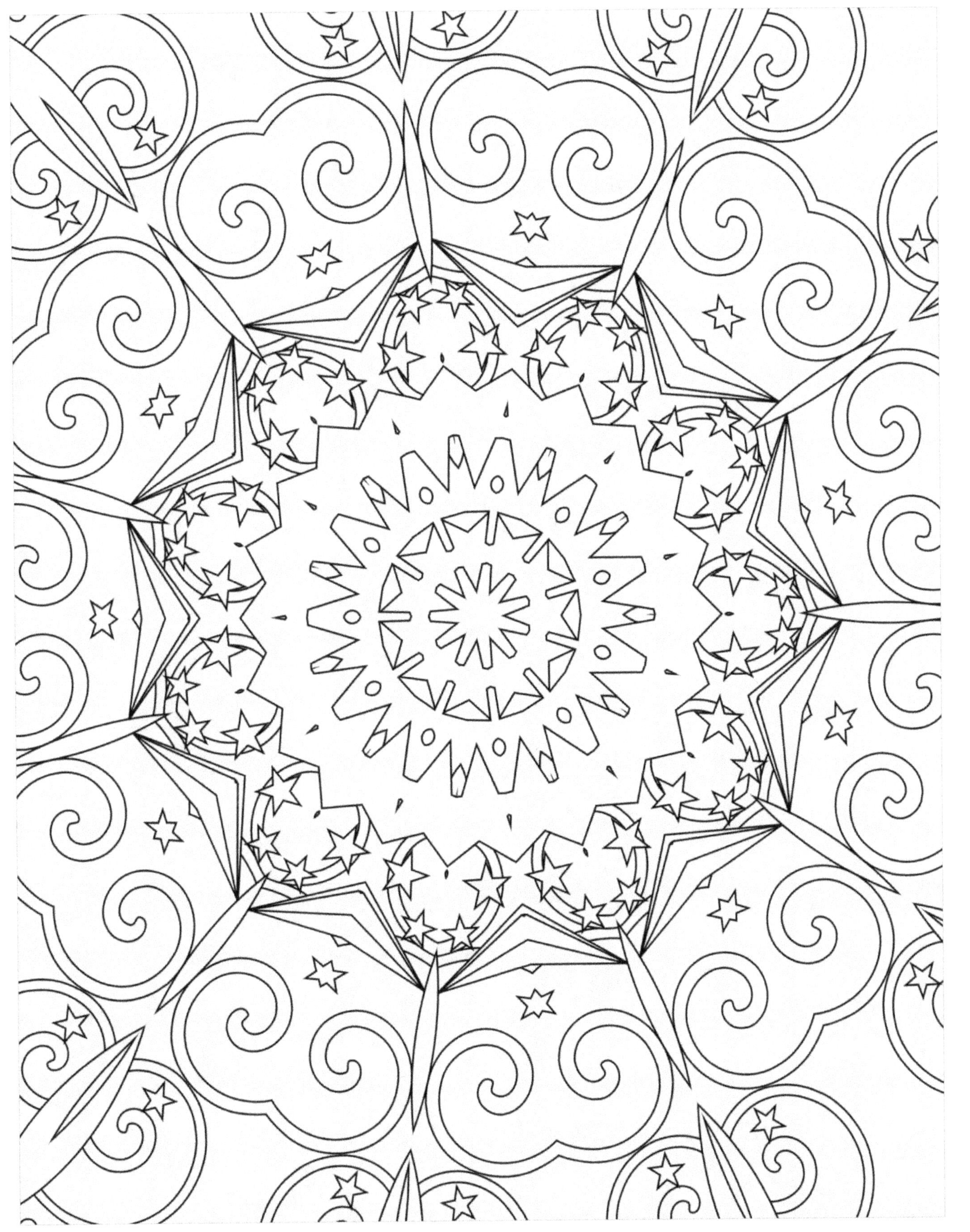

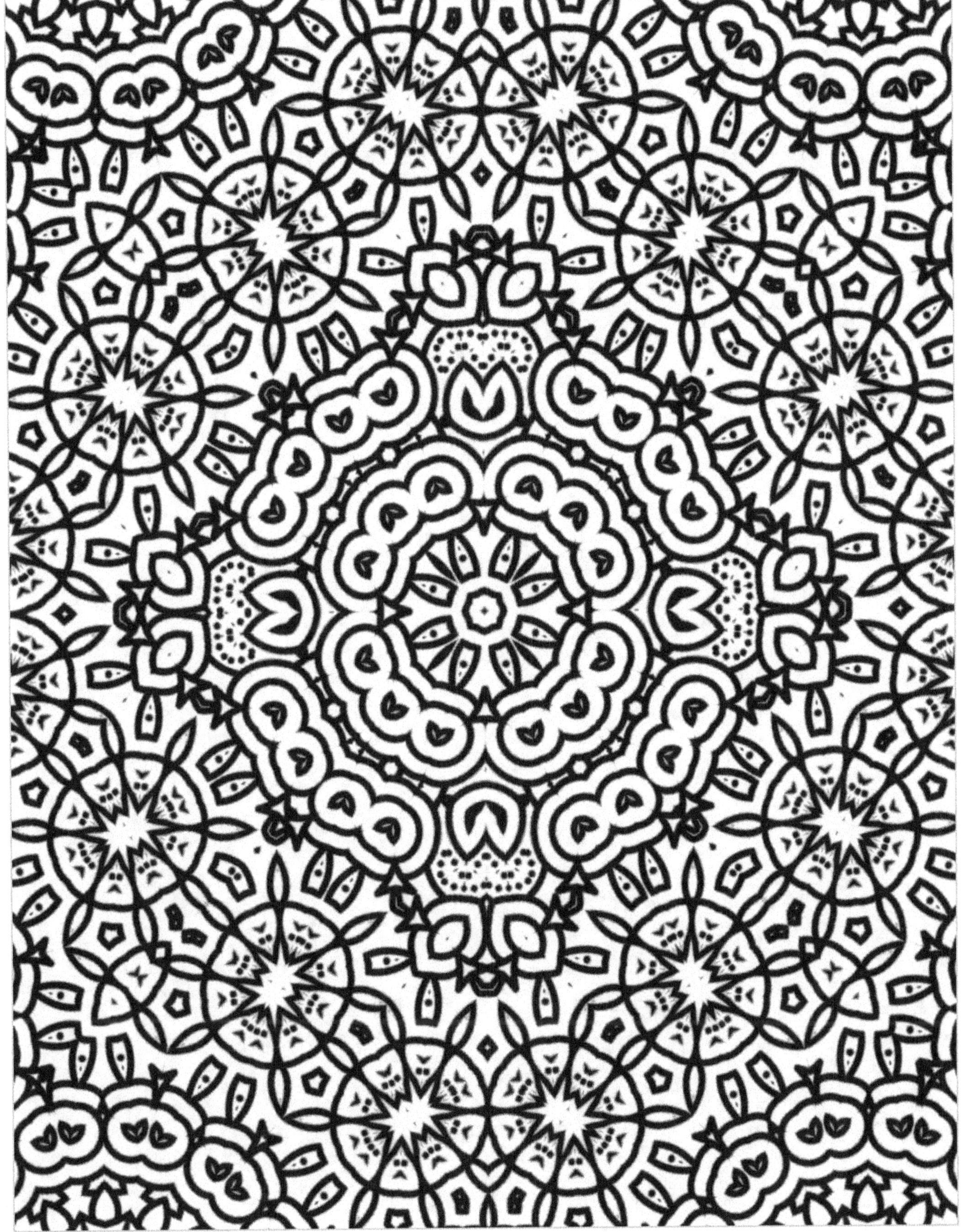

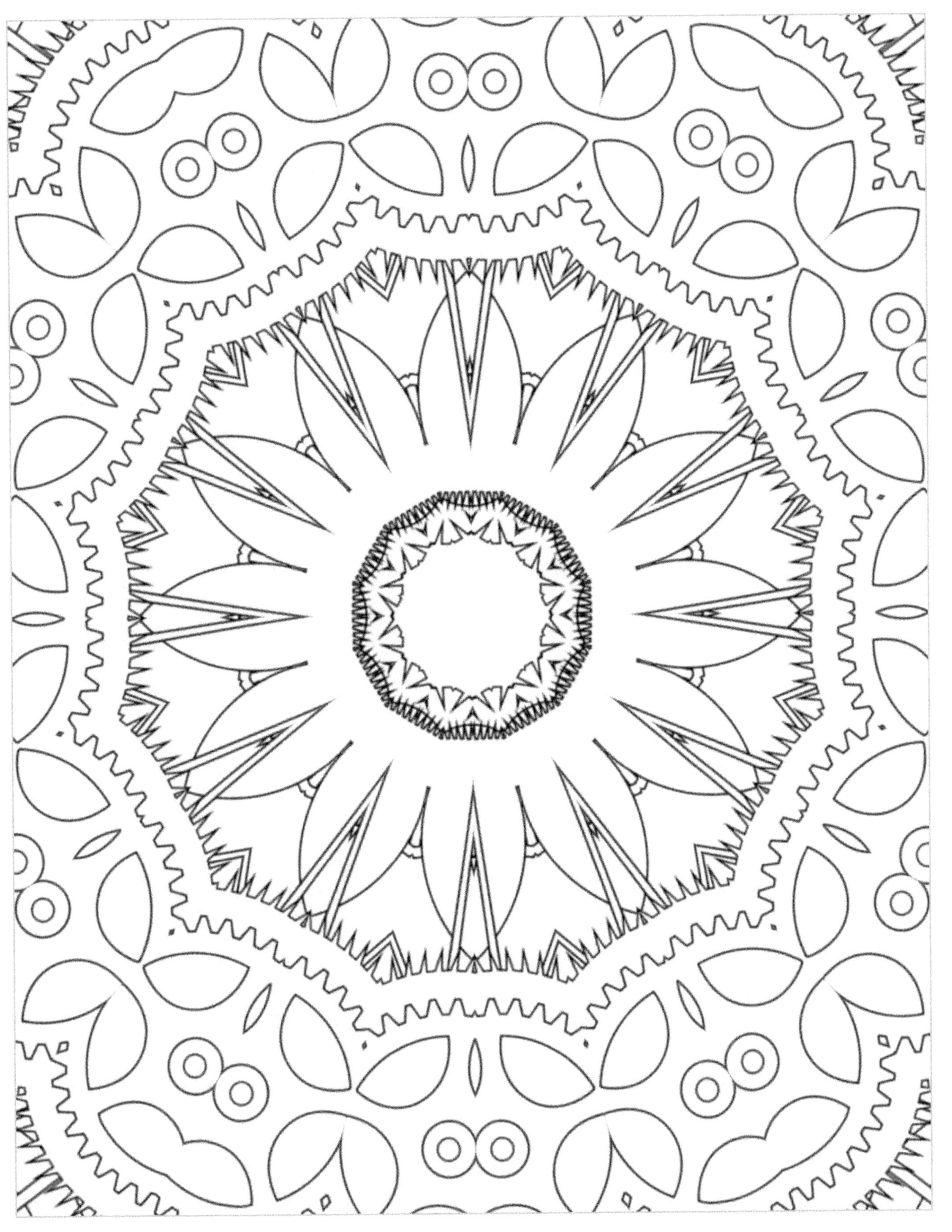

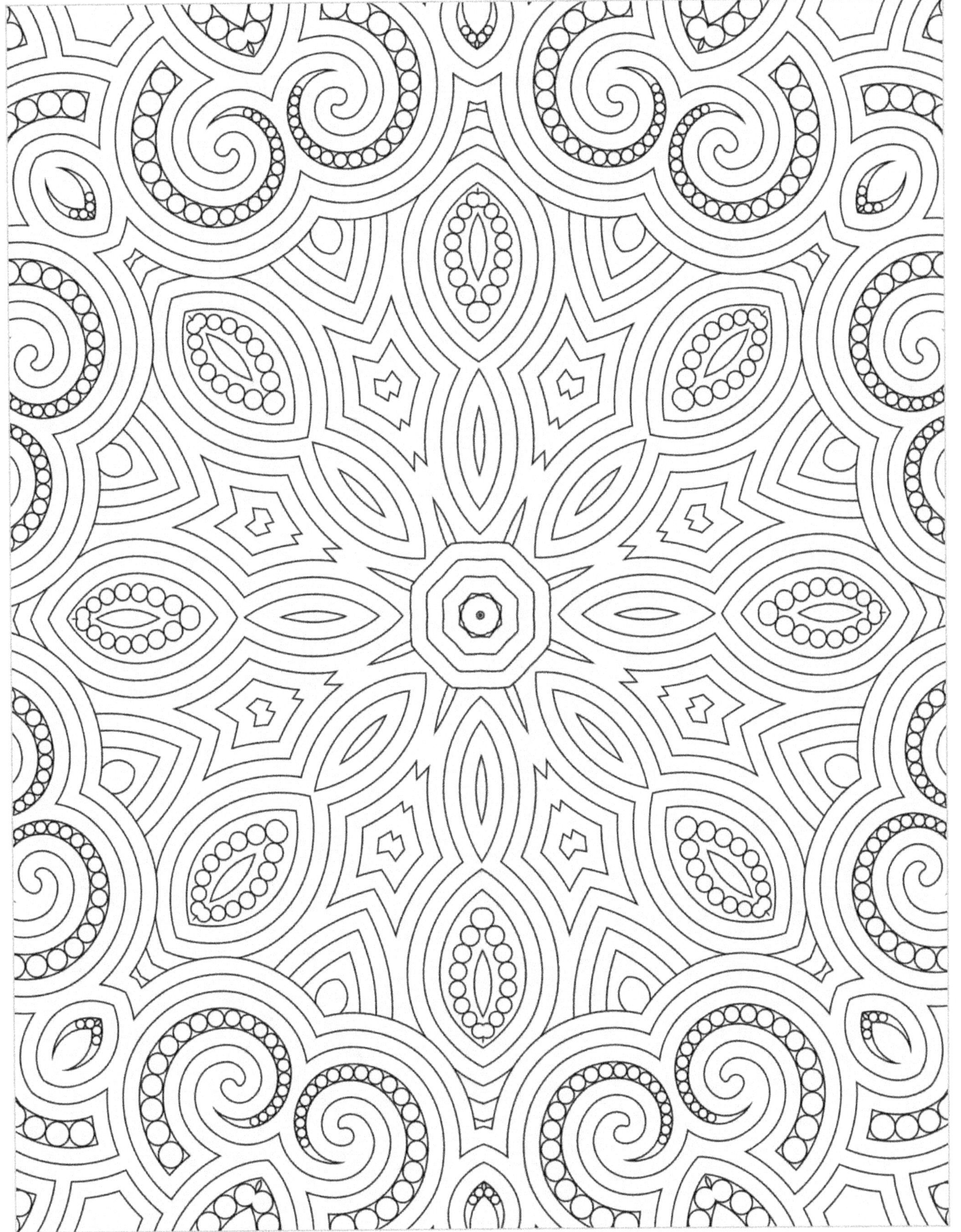

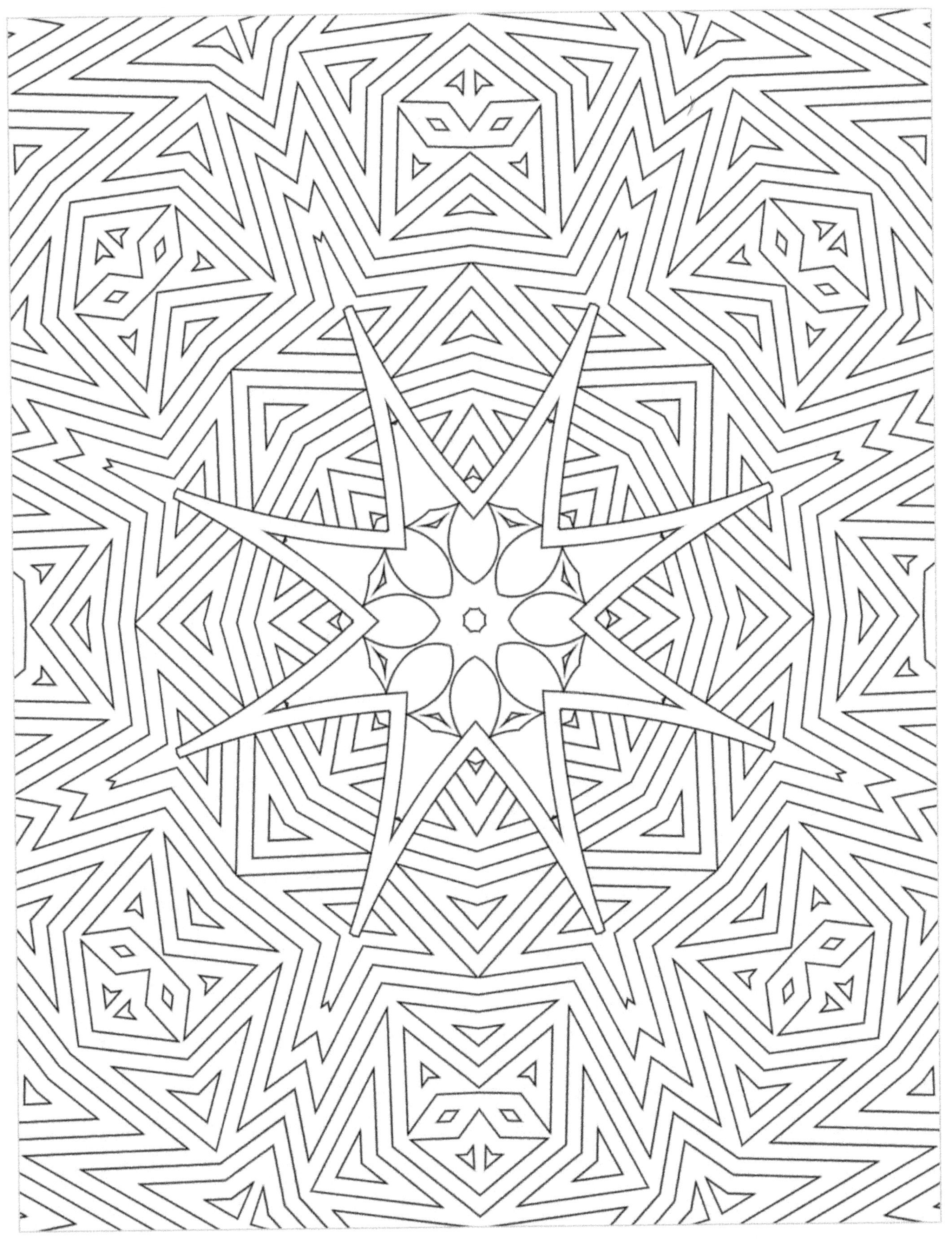

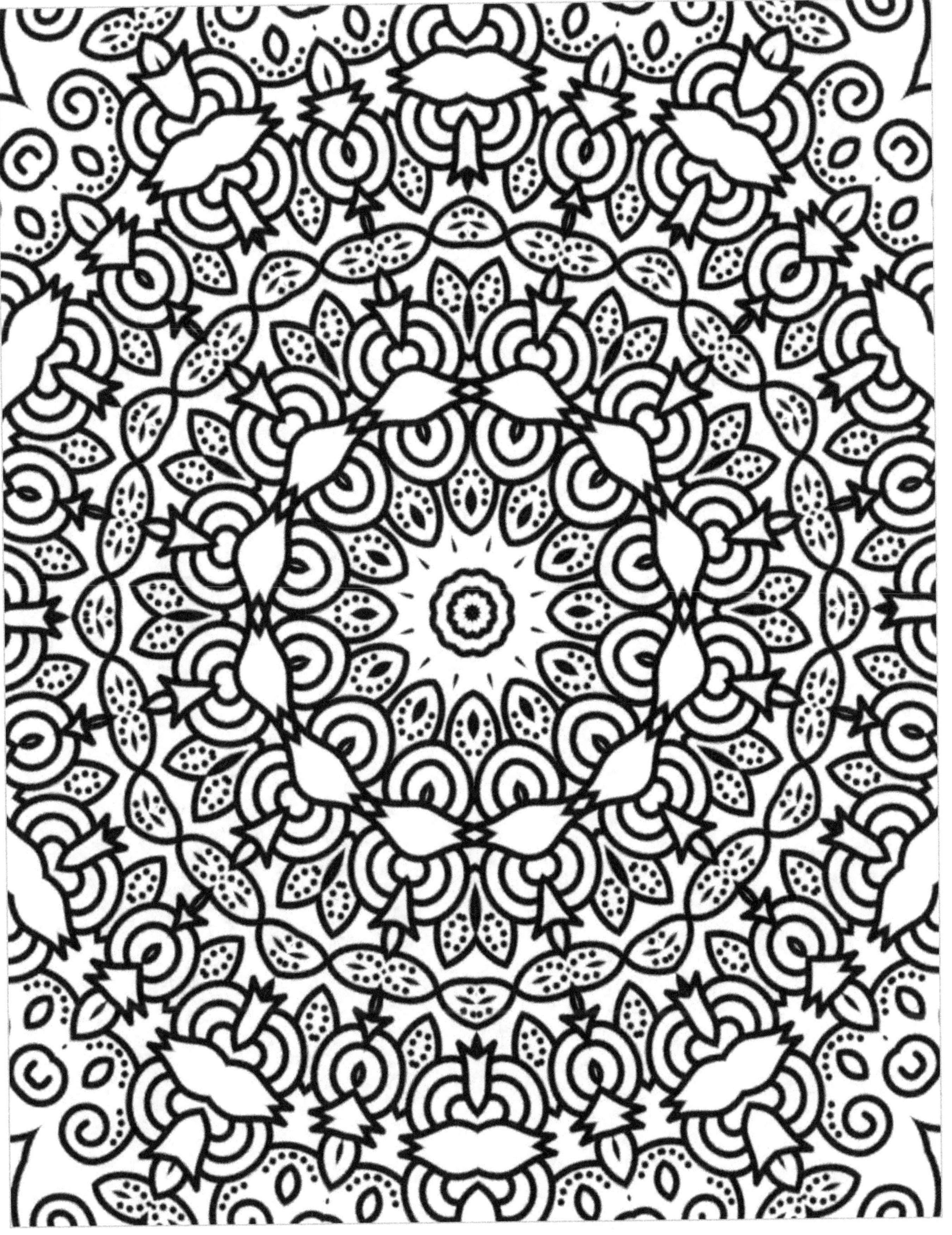

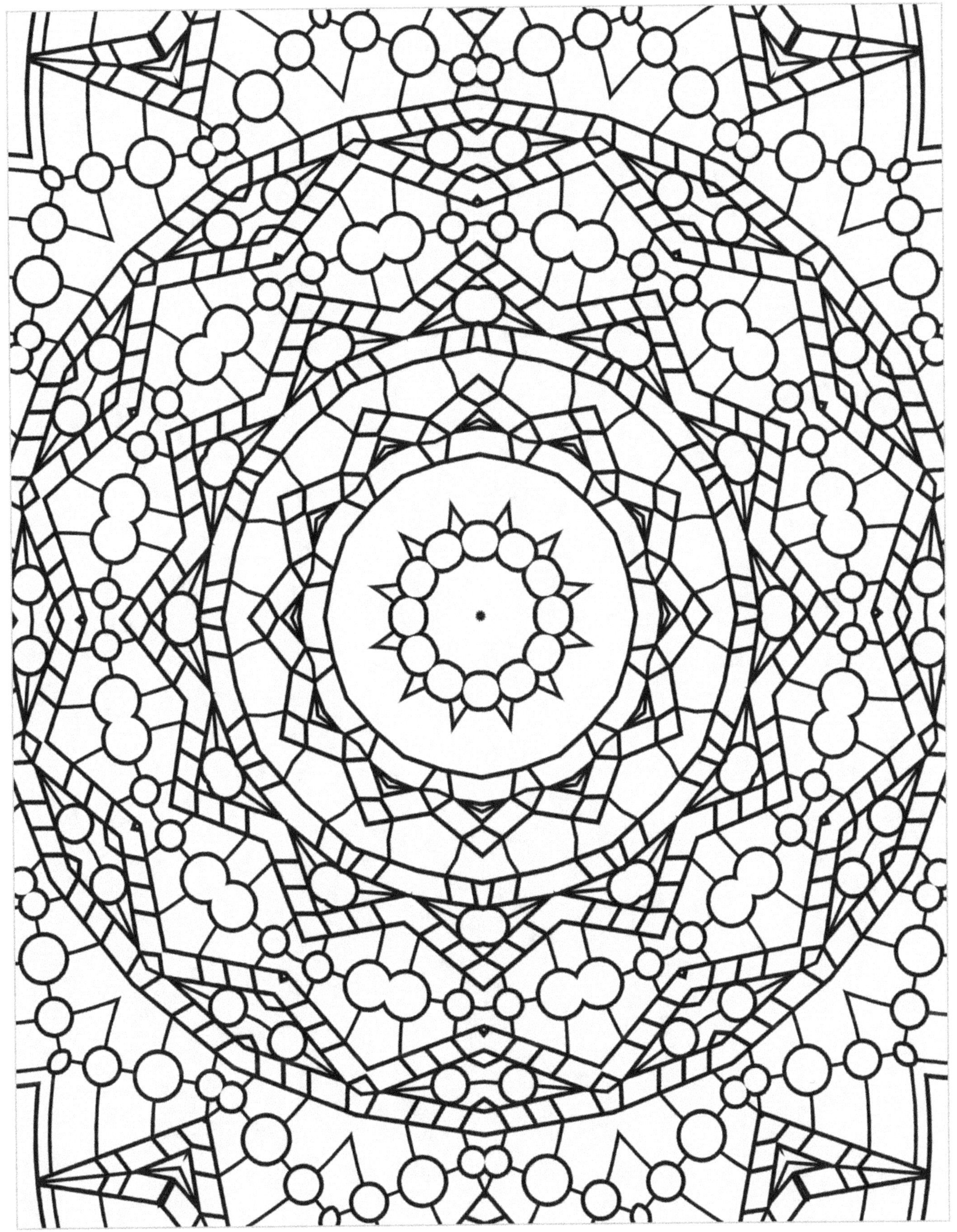

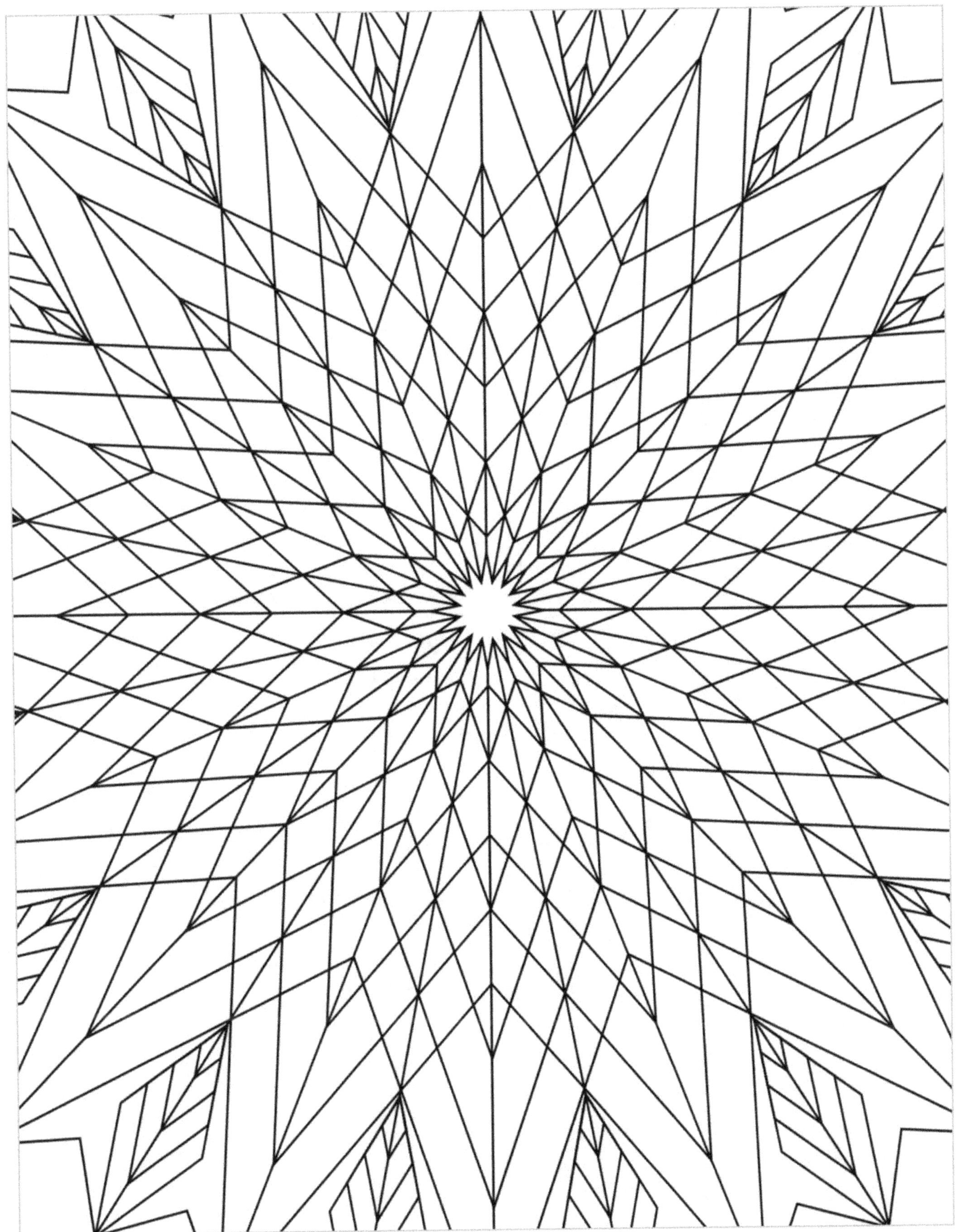

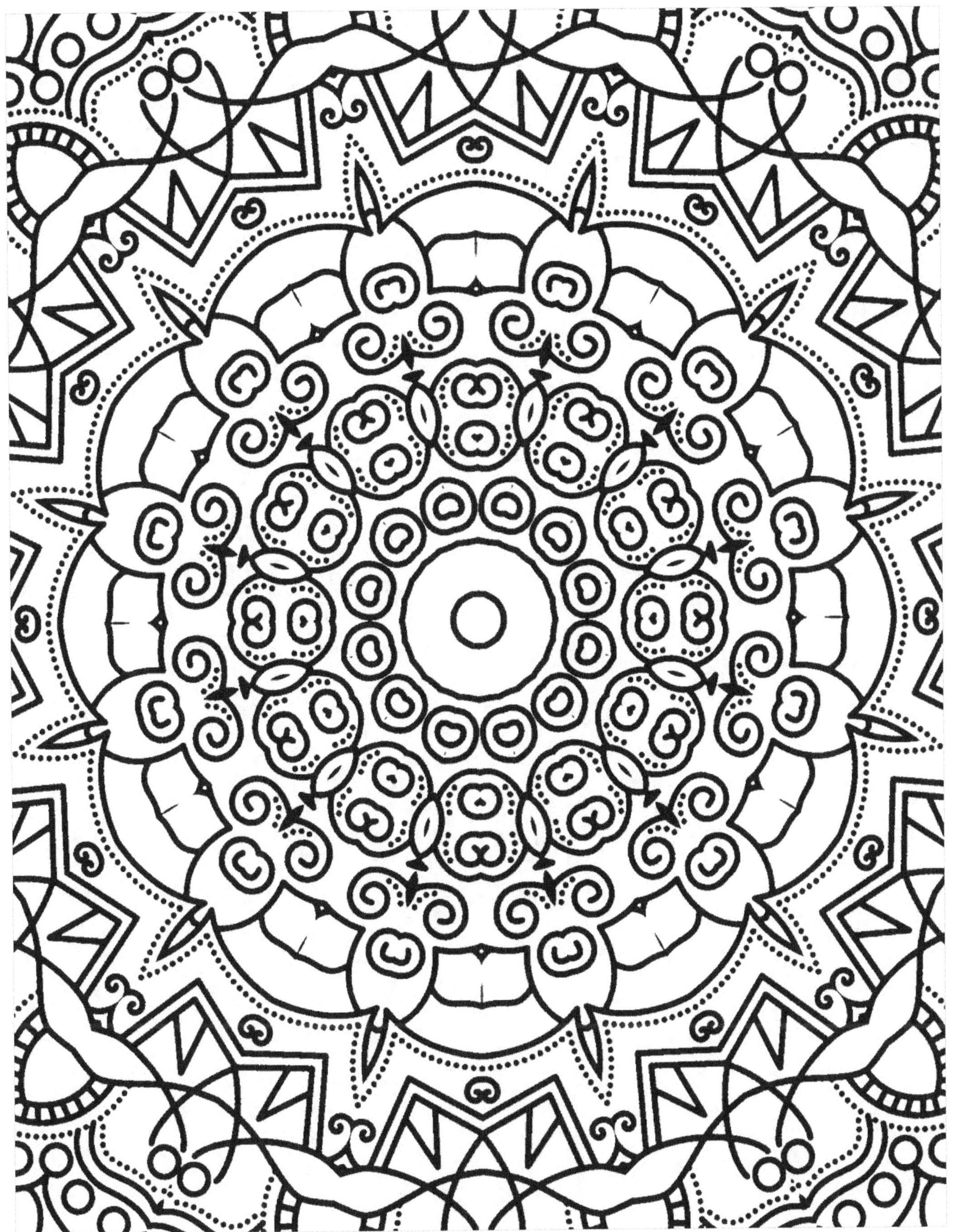

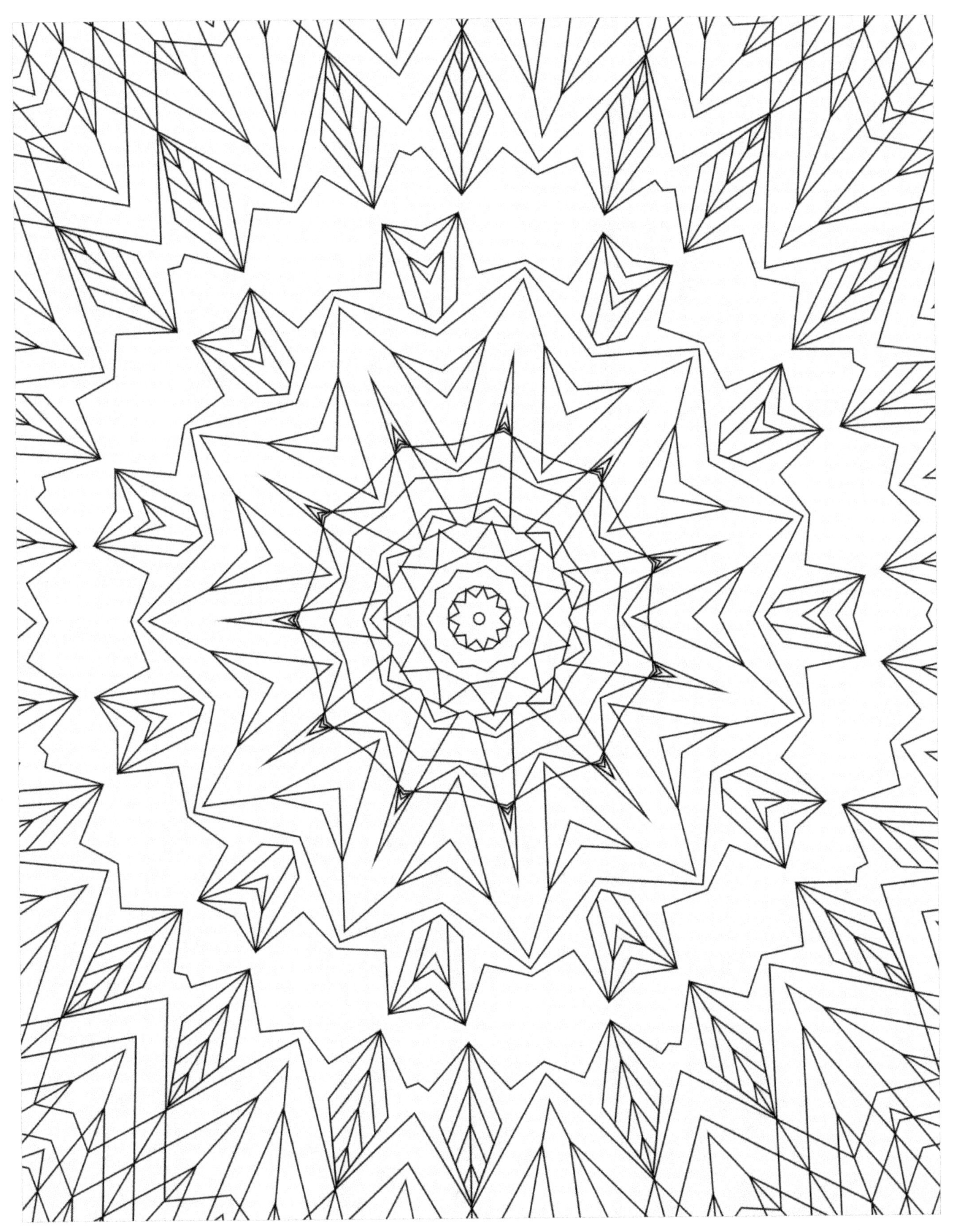

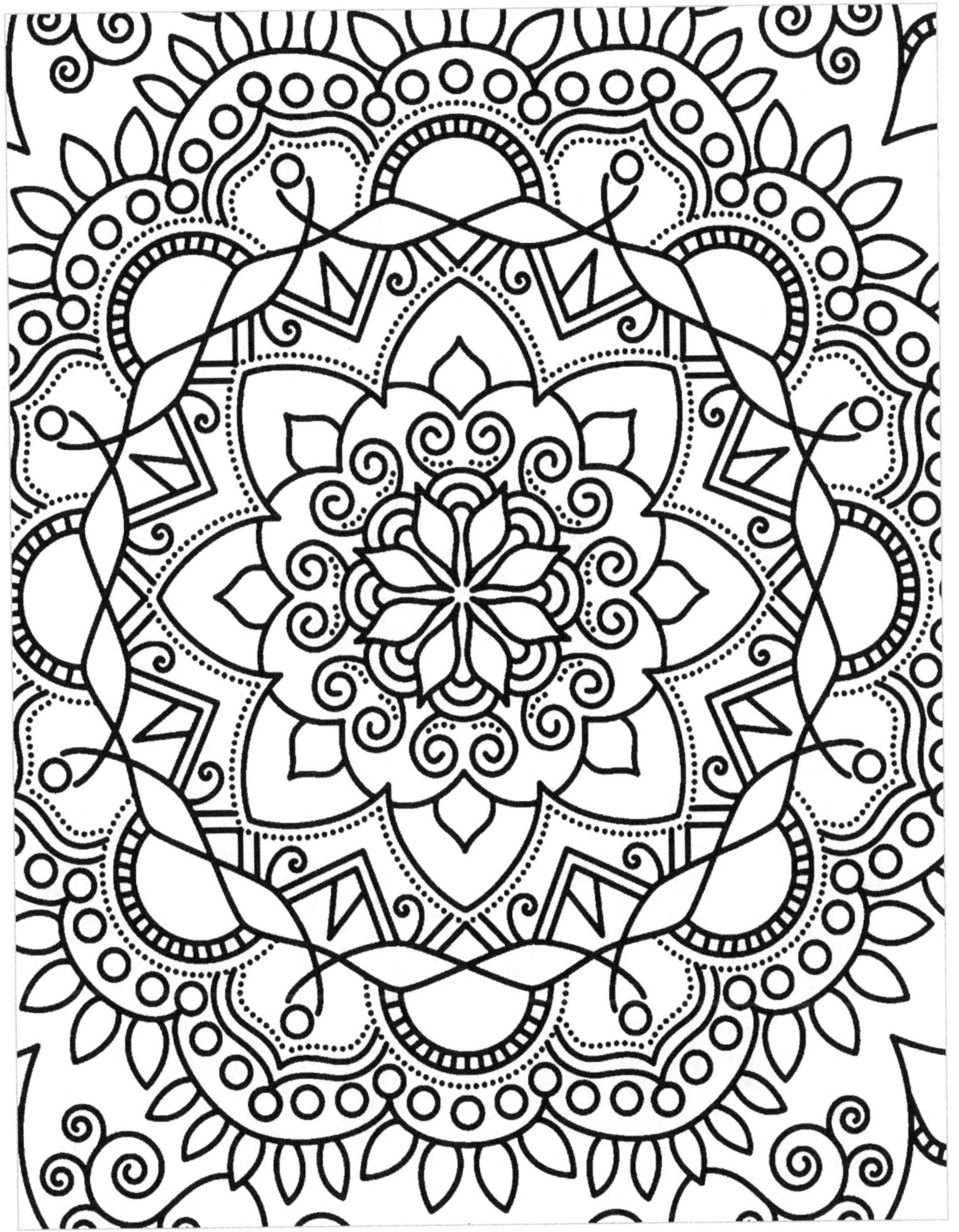

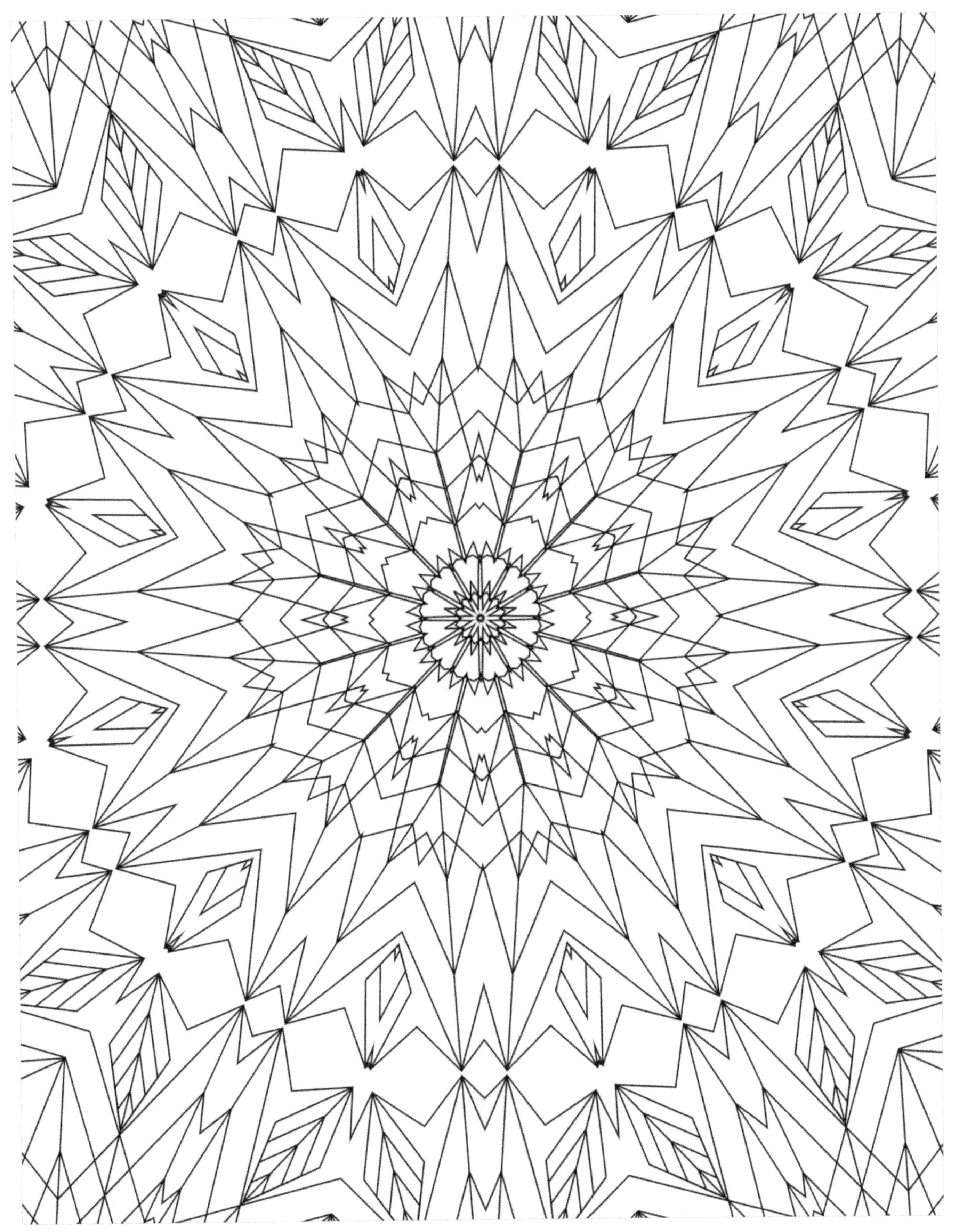

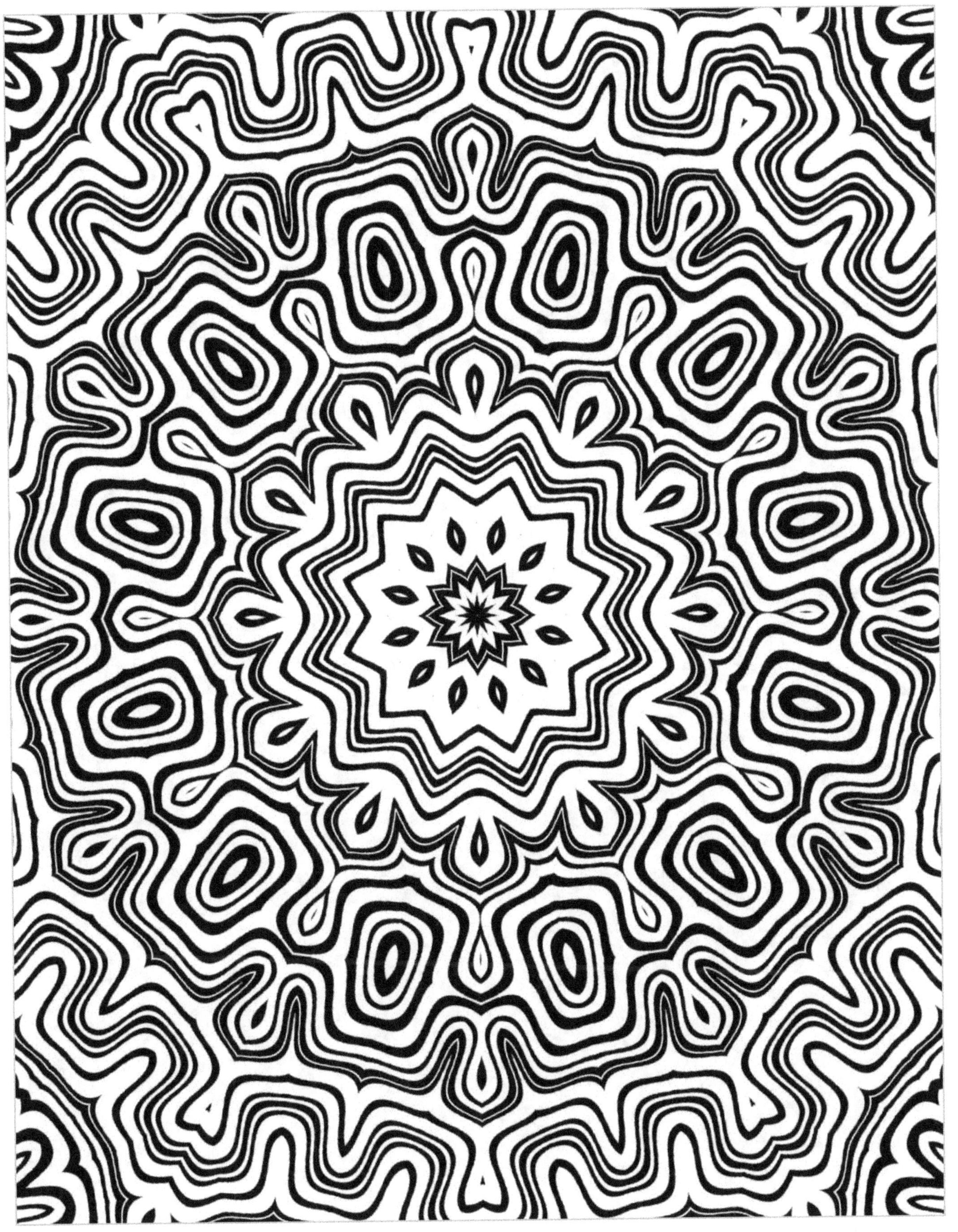

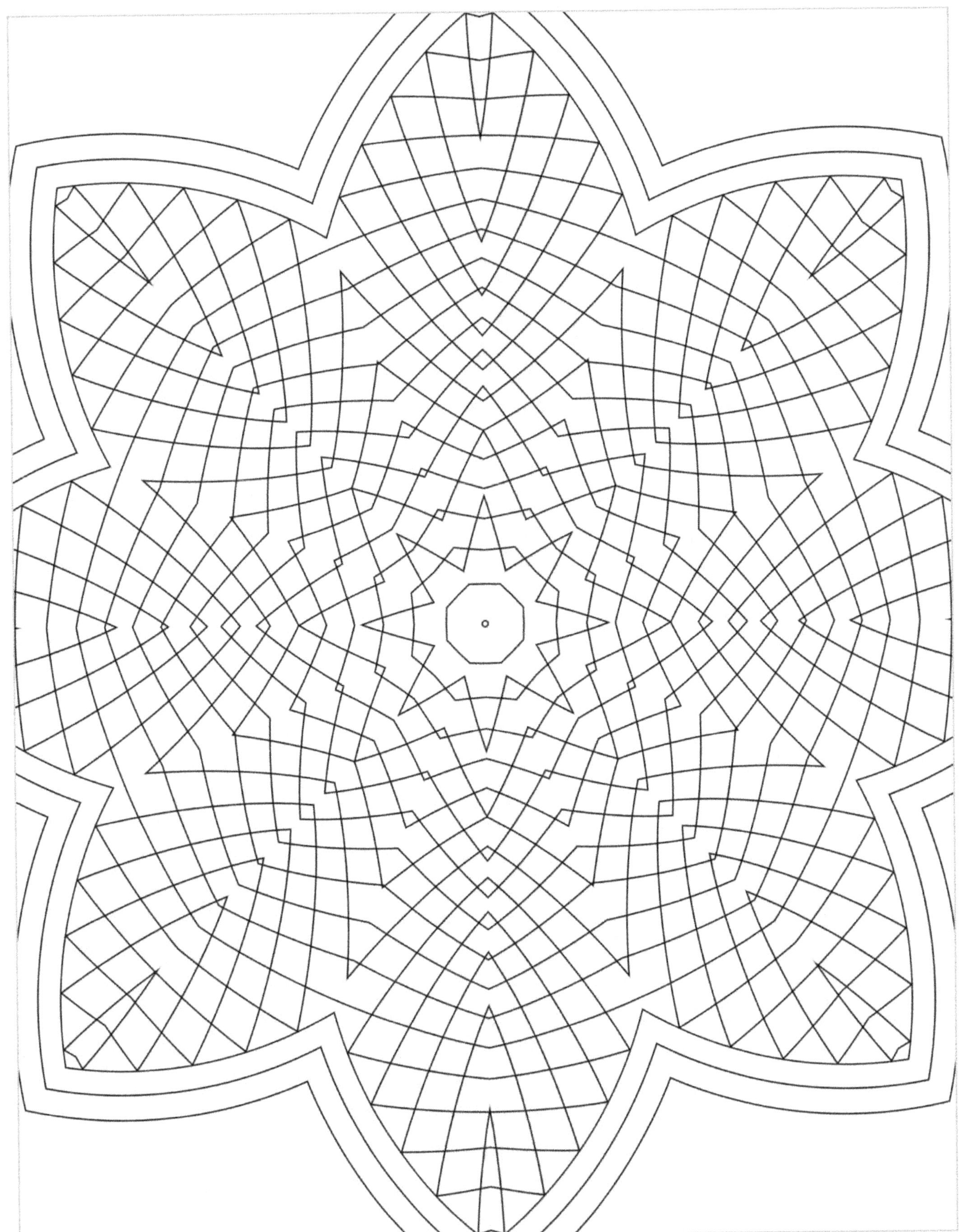

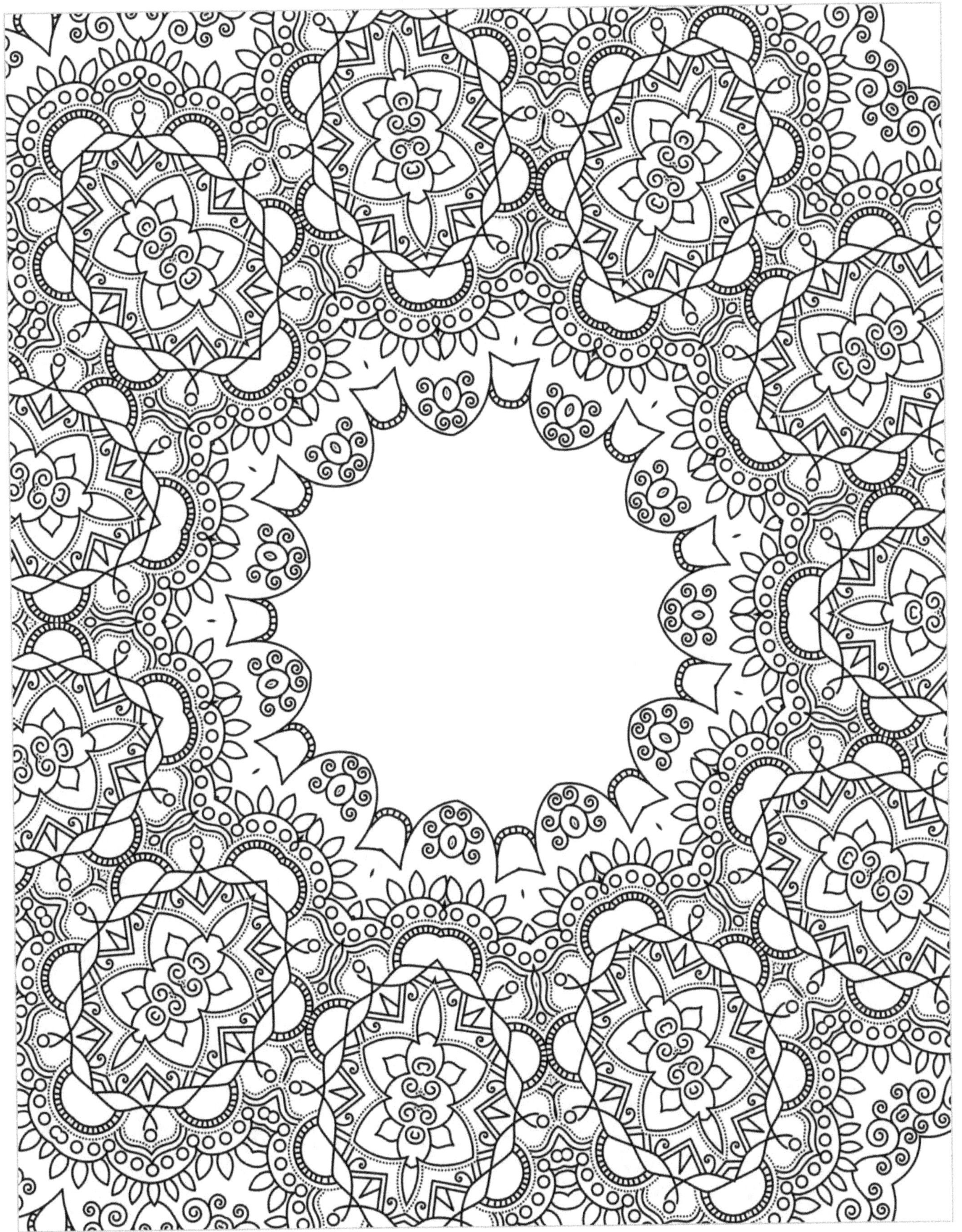

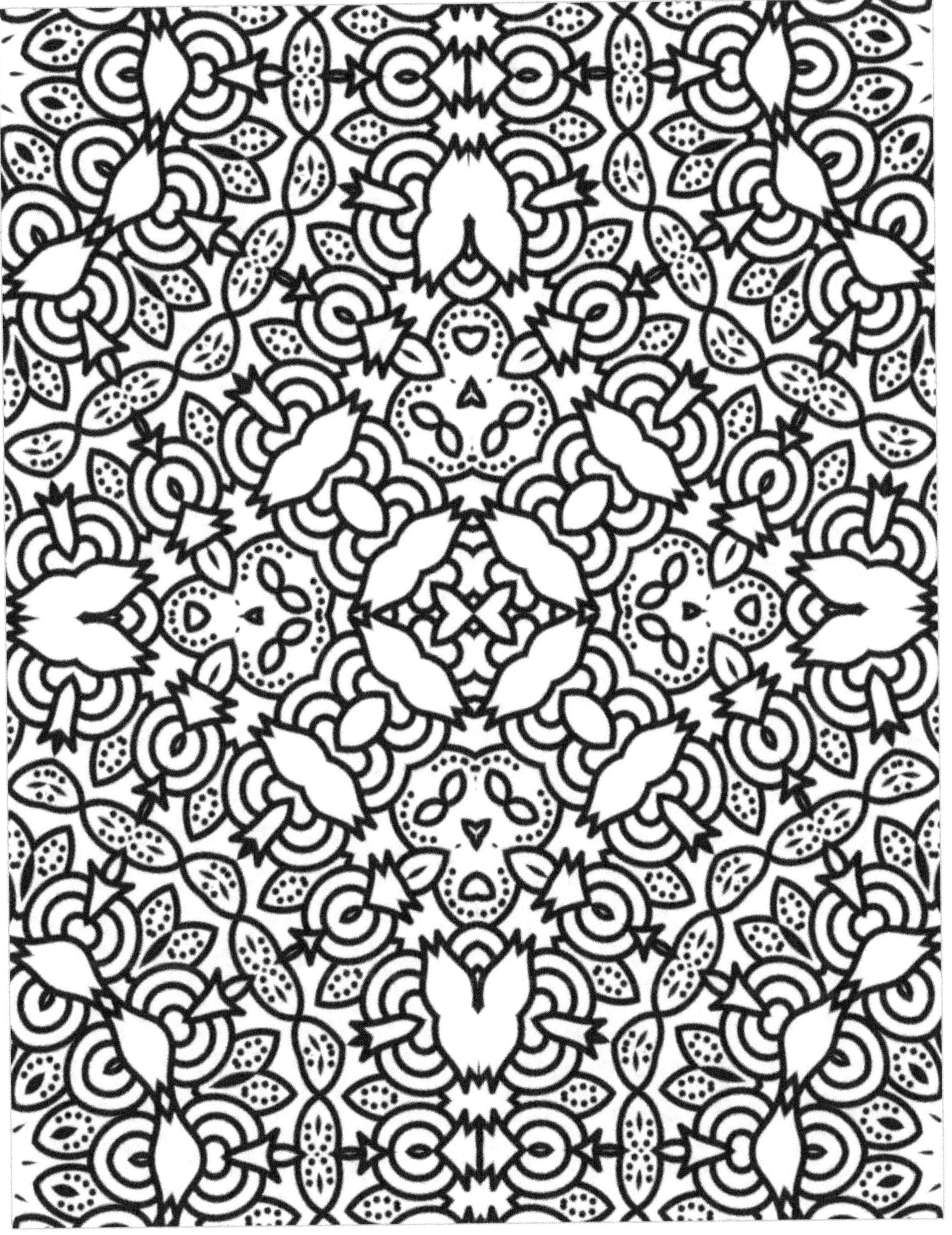

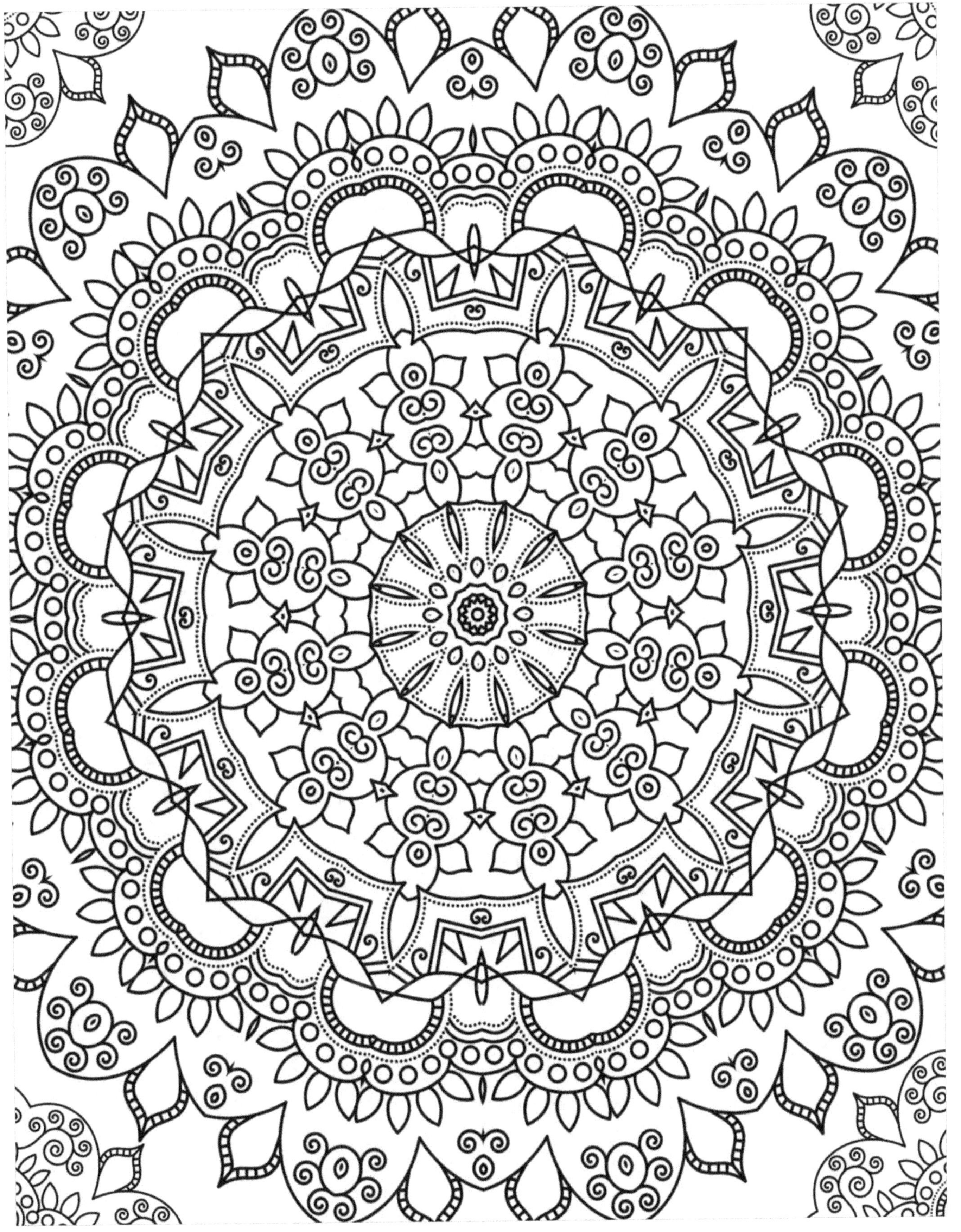

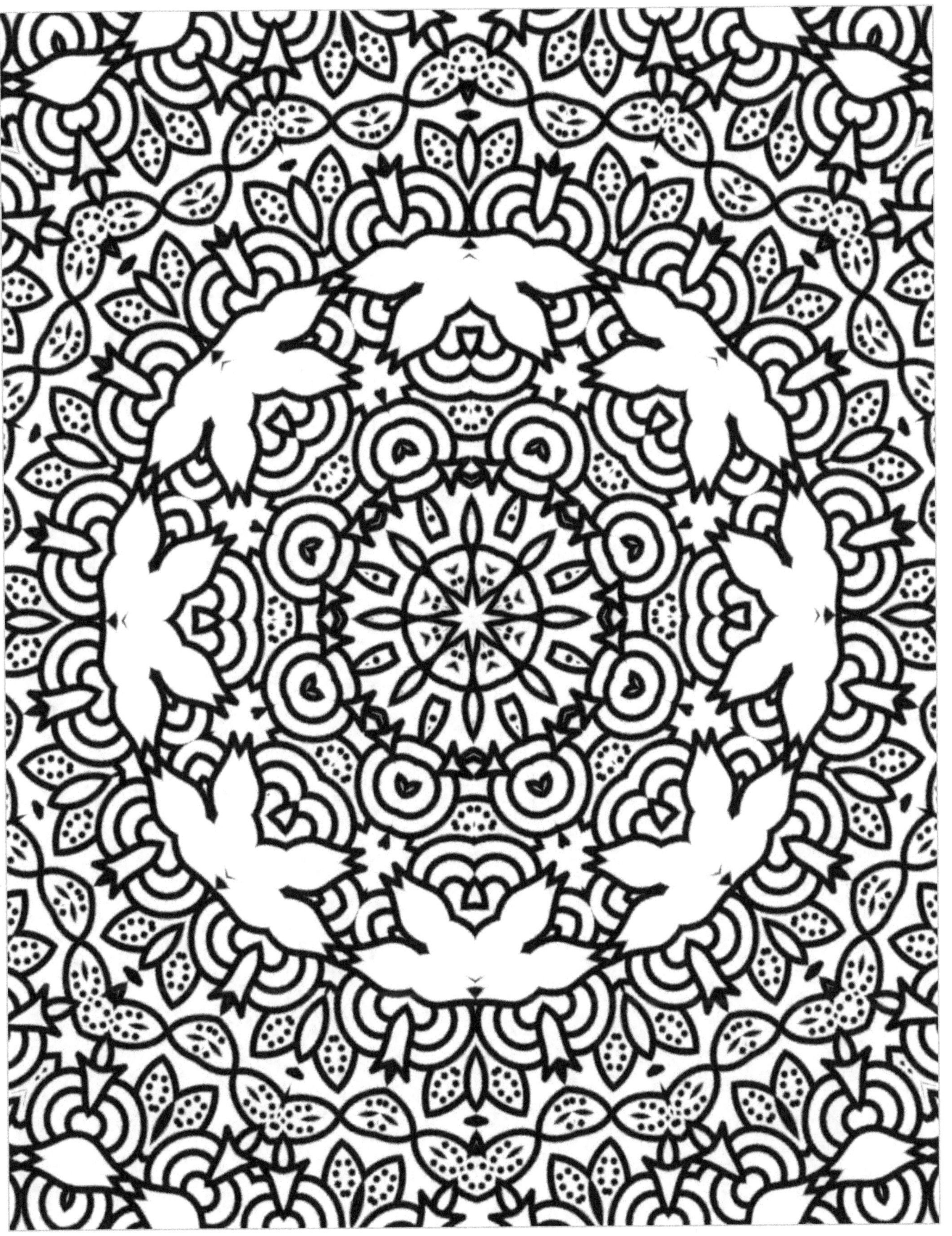

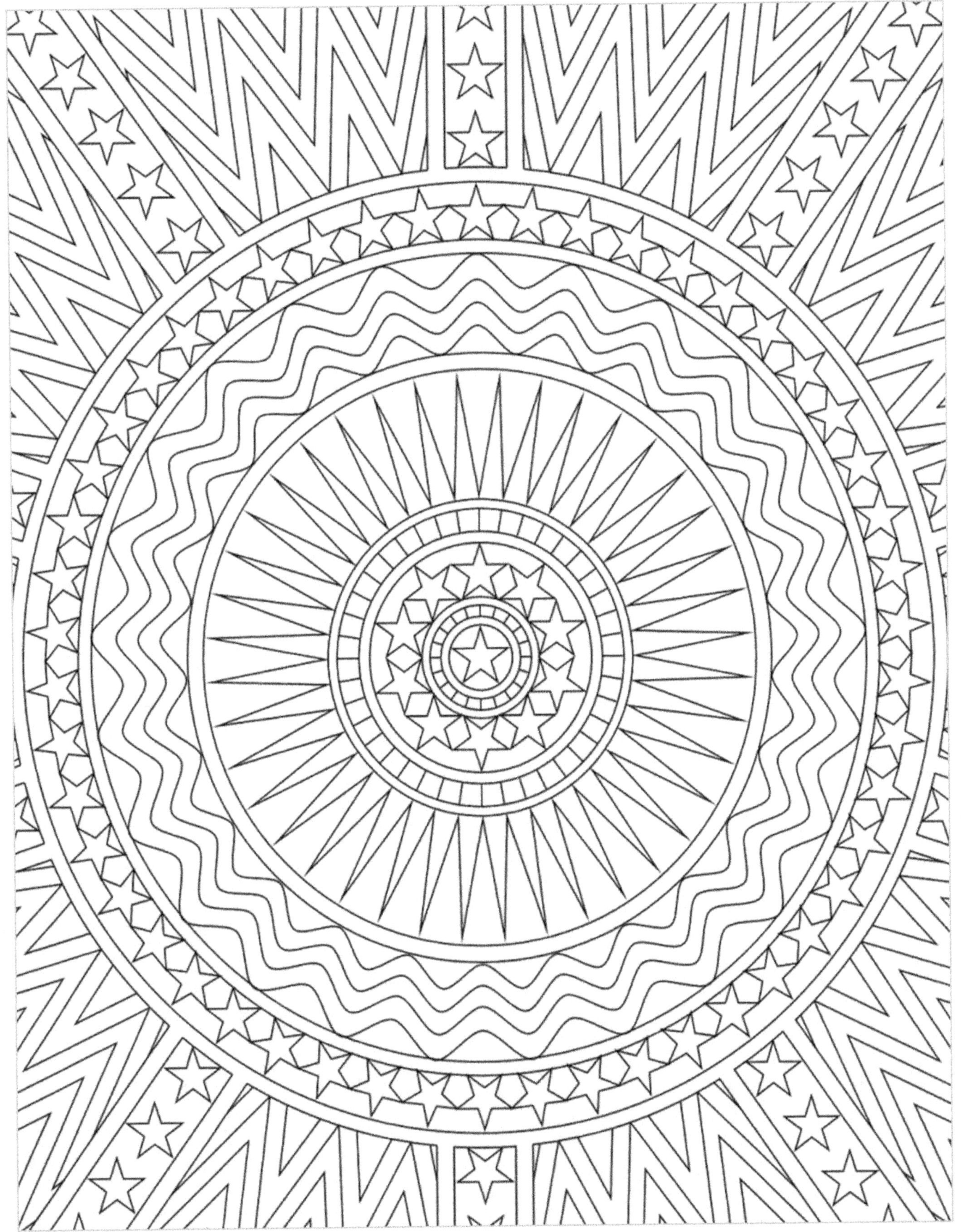

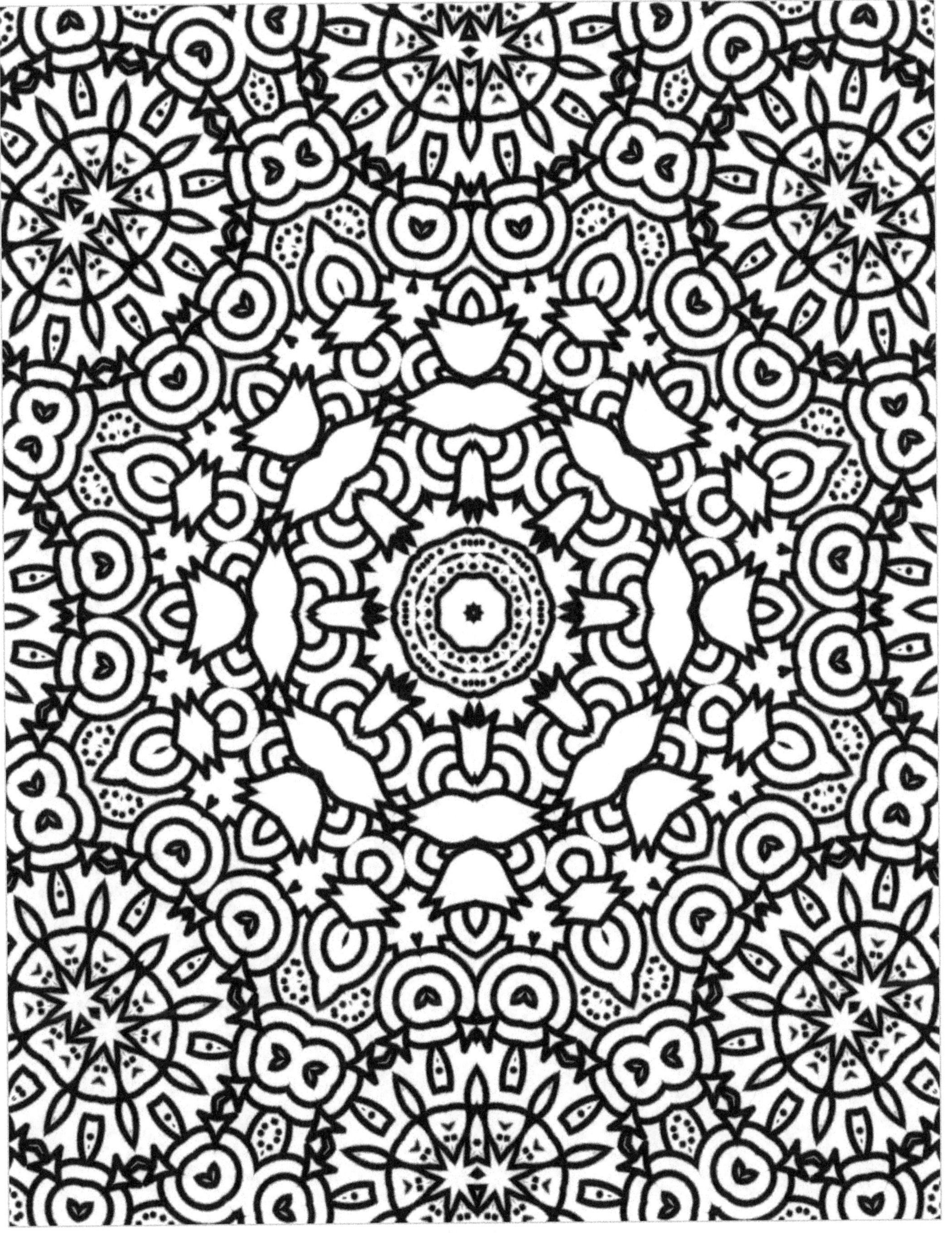

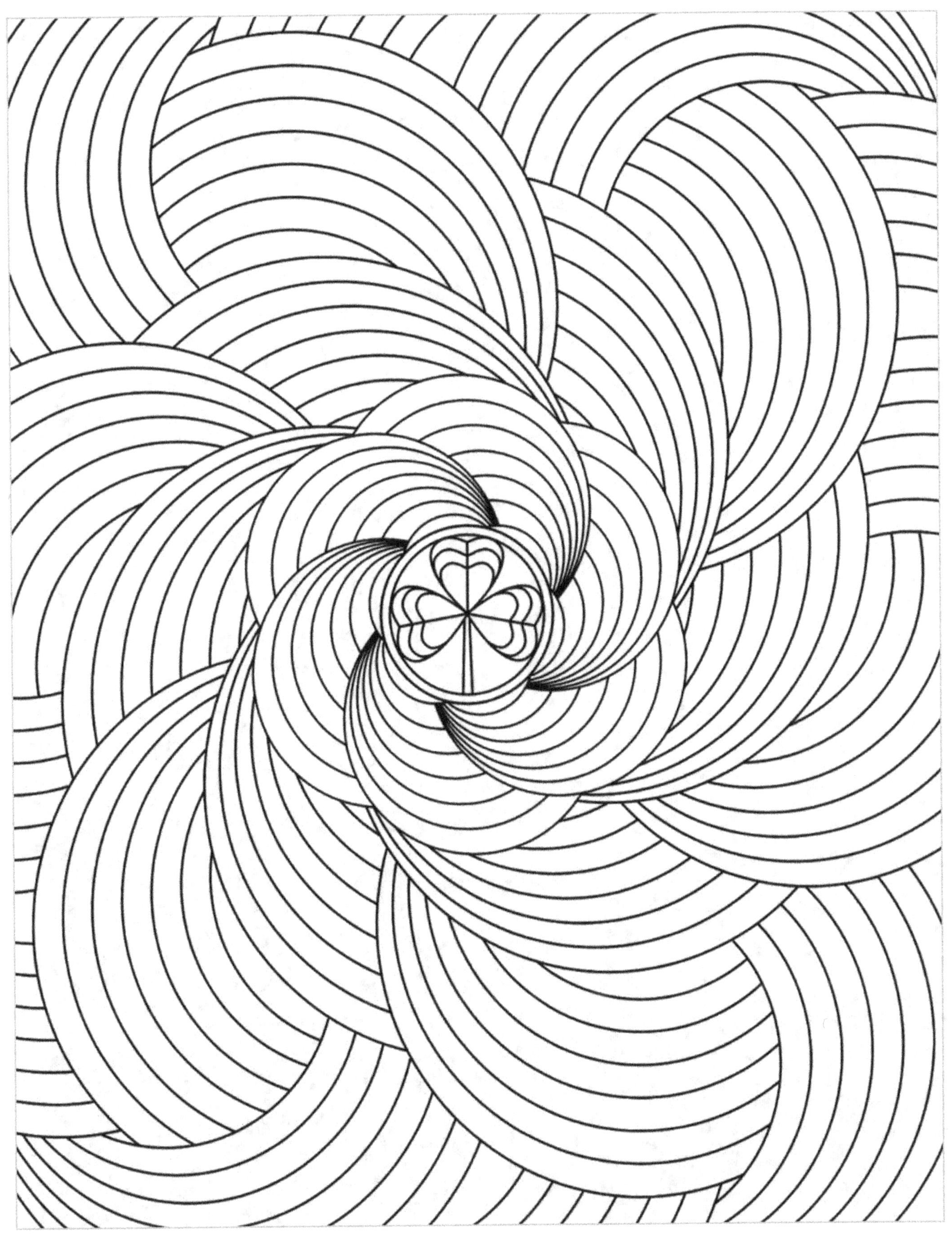

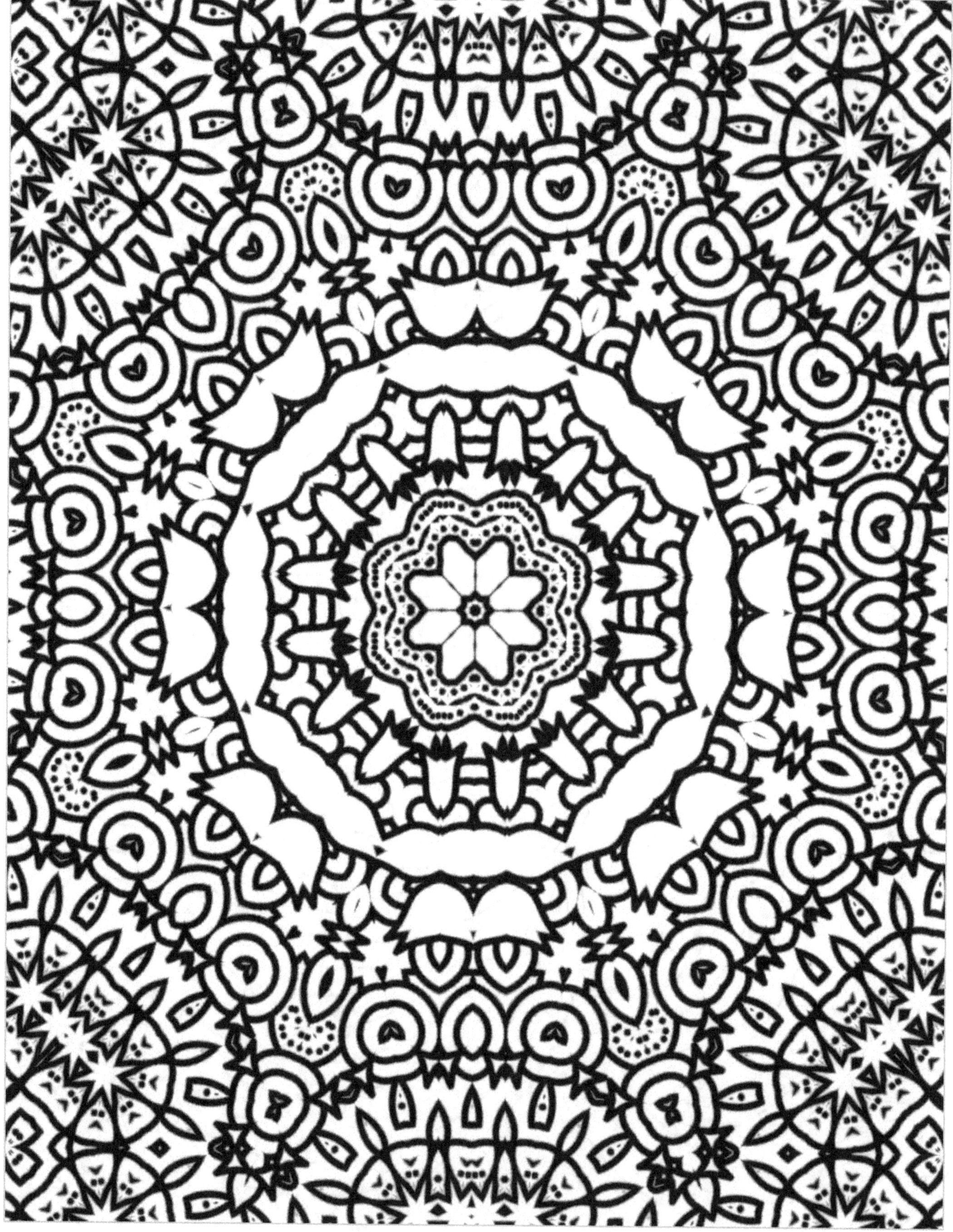

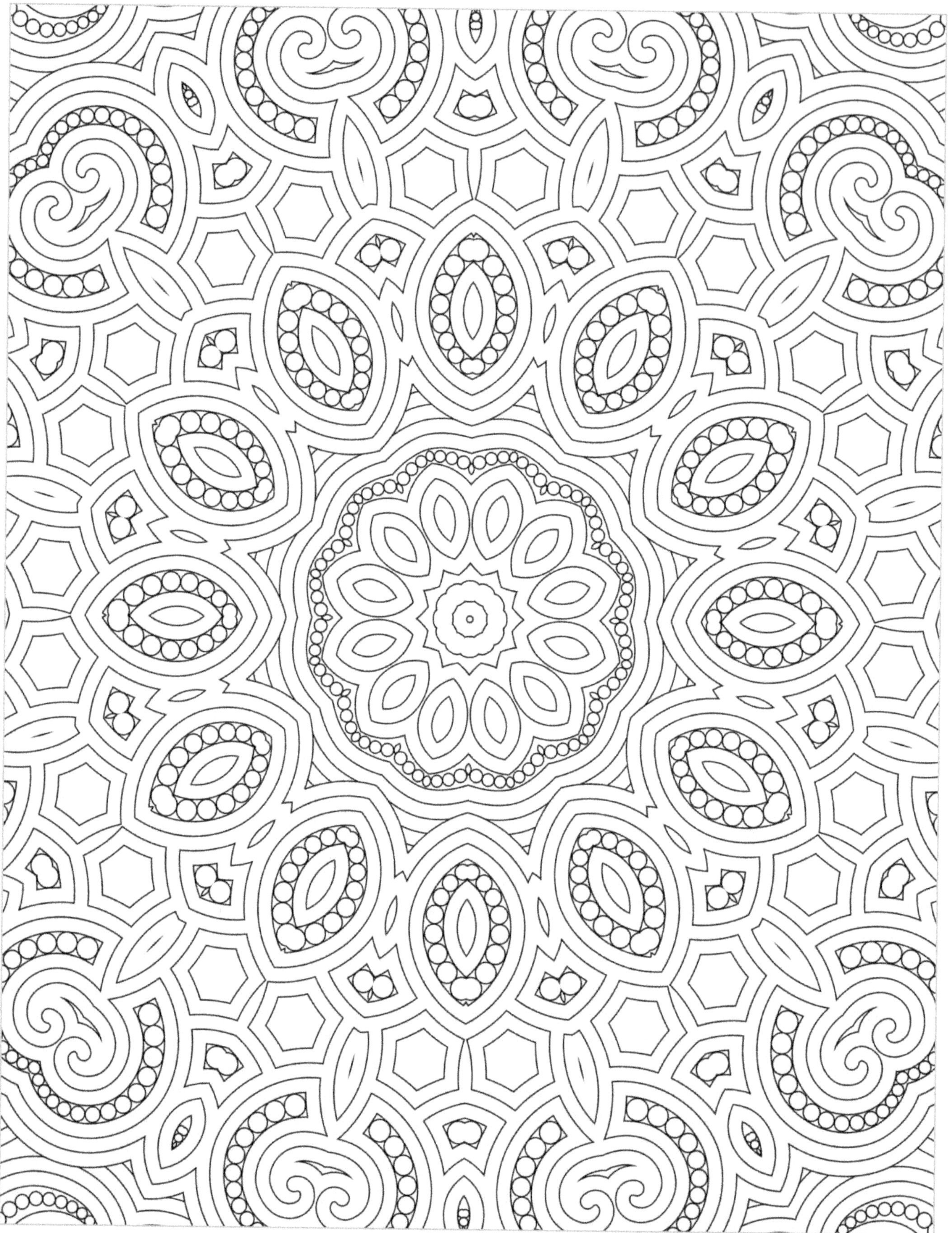

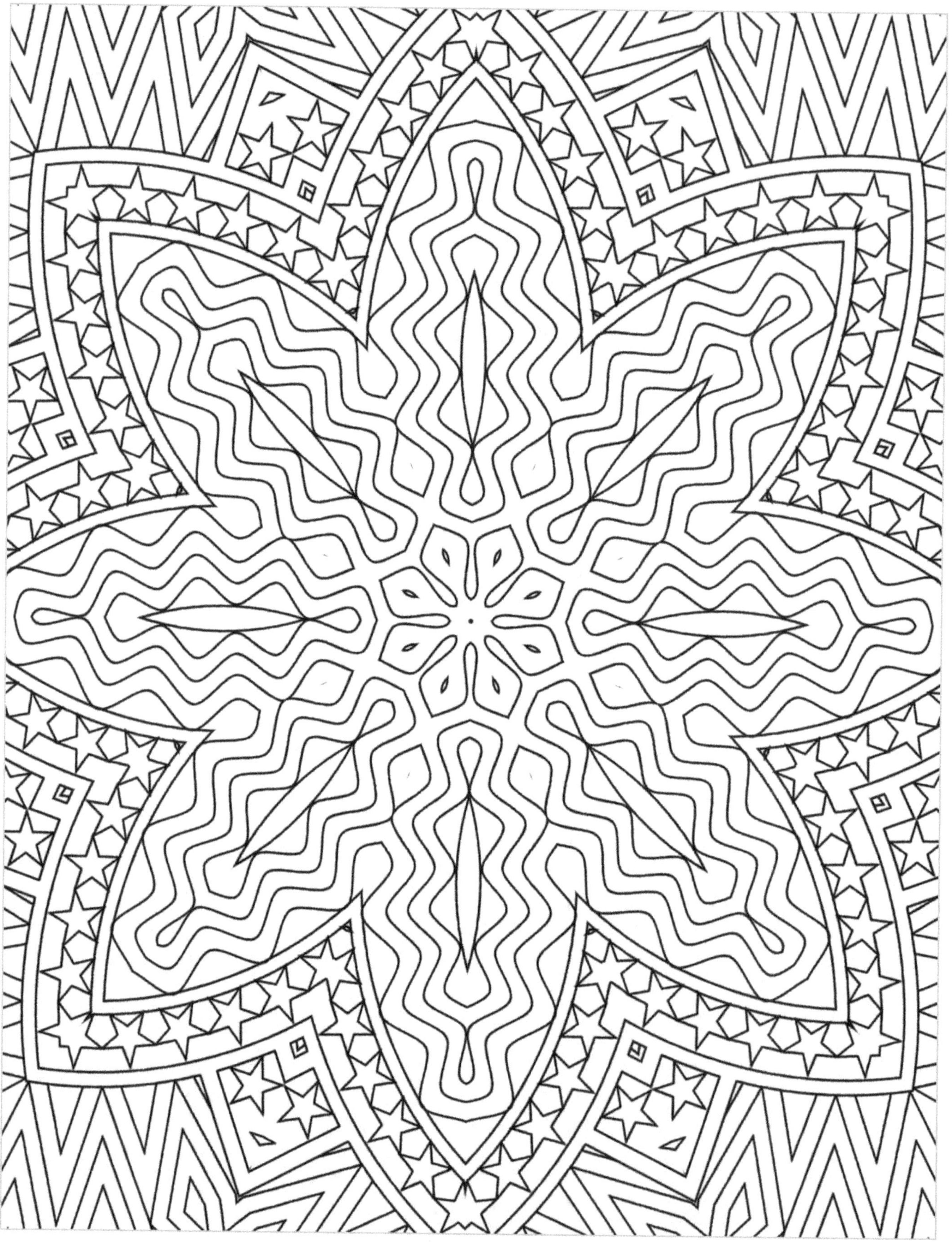

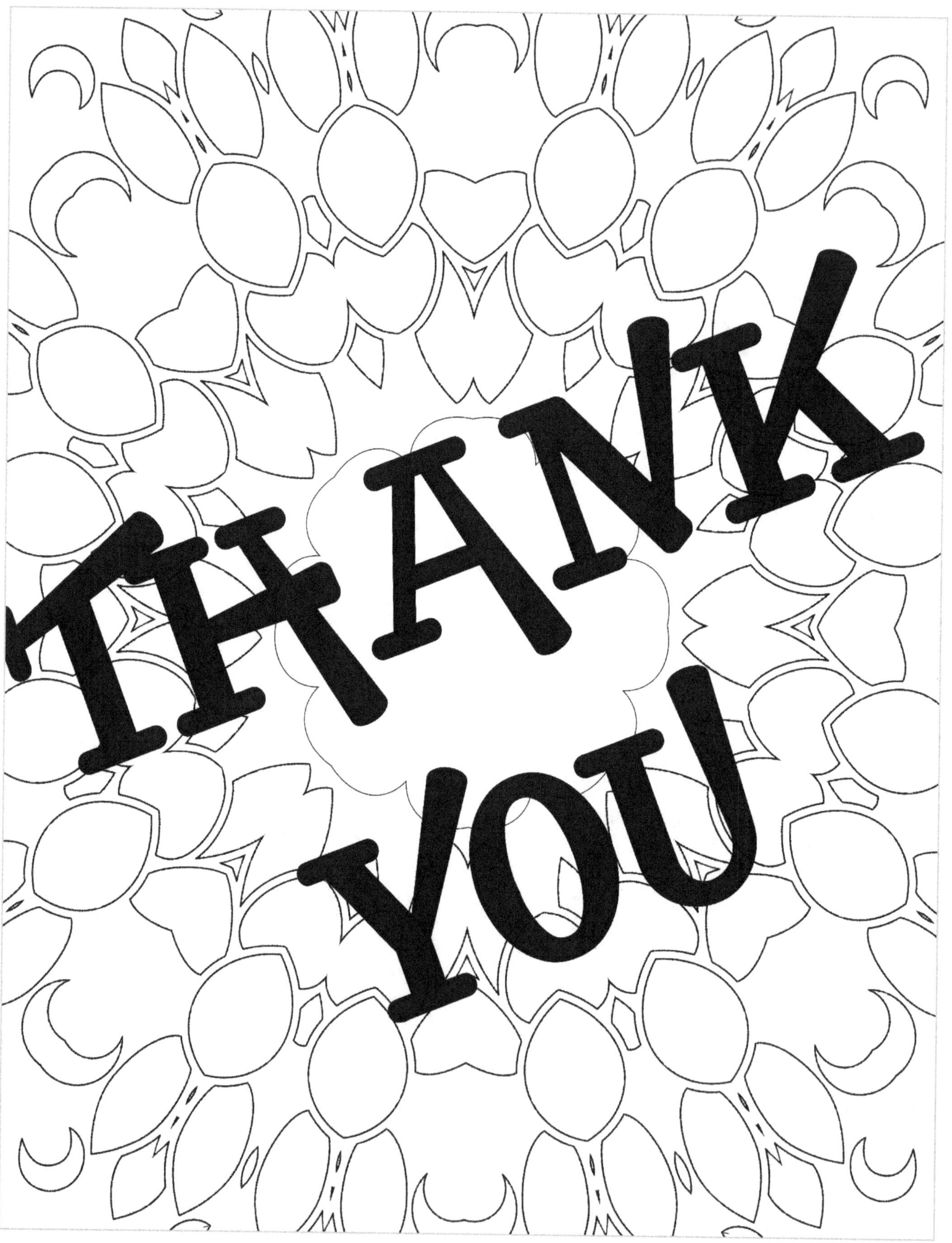

THANK
YOU